BUDGETING

How To Take Control Of Your Money, Reduce Debt And Start Living

NOEL BRADSHAW

BUDGETING

Table of Contents

Introduction 1

Chapter 1:

Personal Finance Management: The Big Picture 3

Chapter 2:

The Different Between Good And Bad Debts.......................................7

Chapter 3:

The Importance Of Having A Plan 11

Chapter 4:

Minimizing Expenses 13

Chapter 5:

Investing In Your Future 19

Chapter 6:

Paying Off Bad Debts 23

Conclusion 27

INTRODUCTION

Personal finance is one of the most popular and evergreen topics for any seminar, book or video course, because we will never outgrow or outlive our desire to have enough money for our needs and wants. And while personal finance is quite a complex and wide-ranging topic, one central topic determines whether or not all the other areas of personal finance can be managed well - budgeting - and that's what this book is about.

In this book, we'll cover budgeting and talk about other peripheral personal finance topics that are central to understanding and appreciating the art and science of budgeting. We'll also briefly touch on what personal finance management is in general as well as savings and investments, so you have a better grasp of the importance of budgeting. By presenting a holistic view of budgeting, the likelihood of you being in a better position to manage your finances will be much higher.

So let's get started!

CHAPTER 1:

Personal Finance Management: The Big Picture

The best way to understand what budgeting is, its significance, and how to budget your money optimally, is to first get a big picture of what it's part of, which is personal finance management. To give you a clearer understanding, personal finance management can be defined as the continuous process of ensuring that you have enough money for you and your family's current and future needs and wants. The "passing grade" for personal finance management is being able to meet your needs.

There are three important terms you will need to be familiar with. The first is "needs." - things that we can't live without, or if we lived without them, the quality of our lives would substantially deteriorate. Some of the obvious needs we have that money can buy are food, shelter, clothing, transportation, medications and other healthcare needs like medical treatments. As for smartphones, it is debatable depending on your personal situation, e.g., work. But trust me, a top of the line Samsung Galaxy or iPhone are not needs because there are many lower priced substitutes, assuming that a smartphone or a cellular phone is considered an actual need depending on your personal circumstances.

The second term is "current": now. Not yesterday, not tomorrow, but today. Your needs now are your most important needs. There is no use in meeting yesterday's needs because they are no longer needed. And while it is a good idea to anticipate and provide for your future needs, it shouldn't be at the expense of meeting your current ones.

Which leads us to the third term, "future" needs. Everybody is on the same page when it comes to meeting current needs. But when it comes to planning for the future, people have differing opinions. Some people take the approach of "worrying not about tomorrow" by being content to just make ends meet, because somehow, they will miraculously provide for their future needs in retirement. Some are simply too lazy to do more than what is necessary to live today, while some people are simply ignorant, and others simply take things for granted. But regardless of the reasons, failing to anticipate, plan for, and provide for our future needs can have very serious ramifications for us and our loved ones.

Being able to ensure both current and future needs are met makes great financial sense, but what kind of life would it be without getting some of our wants? We don't need to get everything we want all the time, but it can be considered a healthy practice to indulge in some of the things we want now. So, if you're able to provide for both your current and future needs as well as your wants, then your personal finance management grade goes up significantly. But always remember that the passing grade - the minimum you should aim for when managing your personal finances - is meeting your current and future anticipated needs.

Cash Flow

This term refers to the direction in which your money moves: going into your pockets or accounts and out of them. There are two kinds of cash flows: inflows and outflows. Cash inflows refer to any activity that brings money in while cash outflows refer to activities that pulls money out of your pockets or accounts. Examples of cash inflows include:

- Receiving a salary on payday;
- Getting paid for services rendered from a second or casual income;
- Business income

- Interest and dividends from investments
- Winning the lottery.

Examples of cash outflows include:

- Paying your utility bills;
- Paying taxes;
- Money for groceries or shopping;
- Buying tickets to shows, concerts or sporting events
- Donating money to charity.

The difference between your cash inflows and cash outflows for a specific time period (usually one month) is referred to as your net cash flow, and it can be positive, negative or neutral. When your net cash flow is negative it means that your cash outflows are greater than you cash inflows for that particular period, or in other words, expenses exceed income. This means you are not meeting either your current or future needs. When your net cash flow is neutral it means your cash inflows equal your cash outflow over a period of time. It means you are able to meet your current needs but are unable to prepare for your future needs. And when your net cash flow is positive, it means your cash inflows exceed your cash outflow and you're able to meet your current needs and prepare for your future needs. Considering that the main objective of personal finance management is meeting both current and future needs, you should always aim for positive net cash flows every month.

This is because with negative net cash flows it's obvious, but with neutral net cash flows you're not able to save money, which you will need to fund your future needs such as your children's' college education and your retirement. You're only able to meet your needs today. But when your cash inflows regularly exceed your cash outflows, you're able to set aside funds for your future needs and wants.

Budgeting

Budgeting has two important meanings. One is creating a plan for spending the money that you earn. It means determining how much you can spend for specific items on a regular basis. The other important meaning is implementing or executing that plan, which is easier planned than done.

Both are important definitions. It's hard to implement a budget (plan of spending money) when there's no actual plan. On the other hand, all plan and no implementation will get you nowhere. You need to have a sensible plan and to implement that plan.

Why should you actively budget your money? If you don't take control of your money, your money will control you, and money is a very bad master but a very good servant. Without a budget, you're likely to spend your money frivolously and recklessly, and by the time you realize it you may already be in a very deep financial hole that is hard to climb out of. But, if you're able to budget your money wisely and effectively, your chances of having all your needs - both now and in the future - as well as all your wants, will be very high. And that means your chances of living a very satisfying and secure life will be very high.

And speaking of deep financial holes, meaning bad or toxic debts, effective budgeting is the only way to get out of toxic or bad debts and stay out forever. To paraphrase a very popular cliché, failing to plan is planning to fail.

CHAPTER 2:

The Different Between Good And Bad Debts

Debts refer to any amount of money legally owed to other people and institutions. Bills that are still outstanding after their due dates, your credit card balance, mortgages on homes and vehicles, personal loans, money borrowed to finance a start-up business or for additional working capital of an existing one, and money owed through other activities such as gambling.

Good, Bad Or Neutral?

Many so-called "gurus" are quick to pull the trigger and judge all types of debt as "evil" or "sinister," and they command their flocks of followers to avoid it at all costs. Are they right? Let's take a look at both sides of the equation.

First, debt is morally and financially neutral by itself. The things that make debts good or bad are the reason for getting into it and whether or not it causes financial strain or stress on your personal finances. You see, debt is like that very sharp set of stainless-steel knives you see on late-night TV infomercial programs. You know, the ones that are so sharp they can cut through steel bars? In the hands of celebrity chef Gordon Ramsey those knives are a great asset. But in the hands of a lunatic they are weapons of mass destruction.

Second, I would advise to carefully and objectively analyze if you really need to borrow money, and if you do, decide if it will be a very heavy burden on their personal finances.

So, that being said, I will now qualify what good and bad debts are. While you may be wondering what this has to do with budgeting, just bear with me and you'll see the bigger picture. Let's start by qualifying what bad debts are. Their characteristics include:

- Payment terms that are very heavy or strenuous on your personal finances; and
- Used on things that you don't really need.

The first characteristic probably needs no further justification. It's neither sensible nor beneficial to borrow money where the loan repayments are almost equal to your net monthly take-home pay or will force you to compromise on your other needs like food, shelter, transportation and health. It will render you unable to fully meet even your current needs, which may force you to borrow even more money and accumulate more bad debts.

You may justify buying things you want on credit by saying the payment terms are so affordable I can barely feel it in my finances. While it may not have a negative impact on you yet, it puts you at risk of making debt an uncontrollable habit, which can eventually make your total debts a very heavy burden on your finances.

Another reason to save debts for things that really matter is because if you continually purchase goods or services on credit you may not have access to credit when you really need it. Debt can be a lifesaver at certain times but by using it frivolously on all your wants, you may not have a lifesaver when you really need one.

On the other hand, good debts have the following characteristics:

- The payment terms are very affordable and not a burden on your monthly cash flows; and
- Used for something you really need; or
- Will allow you to make money.

What is a good guideline for determining whether it's affordable? Firstly, you must be able to consistently generate a positive monthly net cash flow, i.e., your cash inflows are more than your cash outflows. If they are equal or less than your outflows, you have no means by which to pay for the money you are looking to borrow.

Secondly, the monthly repayments on the money you're considering borrowing should at most be 40% of your average monthly excess cash inflows or savings. Why? When you plan to take on a variable rate mortgage or personal loan where the interest rates (and therefore, monthly repayments) change in accordance with prevailing market rates, you'll need some leeway for possible rate increases. While 40% is not a guarantee, it's highly unlikely that your monthly repayments will increase to a point where it becomes unaffordable during its lifetime. Plus, you still need to save money for other future needs, so you need to allocate a portion of your savings for those needs too.

As for using a loan for something you really need, it is self-explanatory and there's really no need to expand on it. But for the third characteristic, by making more money I mean the expected cash inflows from the asset which you plan to buy with borrowed money must exceed the cash outflows related to the borrowed money. Otherwise, what's the point? So, if the loan is to purchase a car that you plan to use as an Uber unit, and earn a second income of $450 a month after expenses, your monthly loan repayments must be considerably less than $450.

Budgeting And Debts

So how are debts and budgeting related? Well, you must avoid bad debts at all costs. When you're able to budget your money wisely and consistently, you'll be able to have positive monthly net cash flows and therefore save money regularly for future needs and wants. By the time a future need - regardless if anticipated or not - arises, chances are you'll have money you can pull out of your savings for such needs. When that happens, you won't have to desperately borrow money and take on debt where it become a burden on your finances. You'll be in a financial position to choose to borrow money at the most beneficial terms or use your own money if borrowing money isn't beneficial. Budgeting wisely and consistently gives you total control over your financial fate.

Another way that budgeting and debts are related is being able to use debts wisely for optimizing your ability to manage your personal finances well. How's that? Remember that budgeting refers to both creating a sound plan for spending the money you regularly get and being able to effectively and consistently implement that plan. The more consistent you are at budgeting your money, the more predictable your net cash flows will be. And when your net cash flows are very predictable, you'll know if a prospective loan's payment terms will be something that you can easily afford to pay. When you're able to do that, you are in a very good position to determine with high accuracy whether a possible loan arrangement will be beneficial.

For example, you have an opportunity to buy a home for your family instead of renting - a home you can truly call your own. Let's say the monthly repayment for a home you're considering buying is $1,000. The more predictable your monthly net cash flows are, the better you'll be able to determine whether $1,000 a month is too heavy or is something that your cash flows can easily handle. If you're able to budget your money well to the point that the least amount of money you save per month is $2,000, then it's clear that the mortgage is good debt - something that will allow you to meet a future need (a home fully paid for when you retire). It will also allow you to save another $1,000 for other future needs like retirement, investment, travel or your kids' education.

And lastly, you will also need excellent budgeting skills to get out of bad debts. Remember, you will need to consistently have positive monthly net cash flows, so you can have extra money that you can use to gradually pay off your bad debts. And as I emphasized earlier, you'll need excellent budgeting skills to consistently pull that off. If you don't have excess money at the end of each month, what will you use to pay off your debts?

CHAPTER 3:

The Importance Of Having A Plan

There are three ways people budget their money. The first is not budgeting at all! They just spend money mindlessly, not giving any thought to whether they are able to save money for future needs. If not planning is planning to fail, then not budgeting is budgeting for financial failure.

The second way people budget is by budgeting their expenses to fit their budget. Only if there's extra at the end of the month will they put something in their savings account for future needs. And if there's none at the end of the month there's no savings. This is called the contingent savings approach, a sample of which can be found in Annex A.

While this approach seems to work for most people, this is neither the wisest nor the most effective way to achieve your financial goals. Why? Remember the main objective of personal finance management is to ensure both current and future needs are met. This is a contingent approach to saving money, i.e., a person only gets to set aside funds for future anticipated and unanticipated needs if, by chance, there's something left over.

The third way is the wisest and the most effective way to budget. Under this approach, a person decides to commit to saving a fixed amount of money every month. They put aside this amount first, and whatever is left is for spending. Under this approach, saving money isn't a contingent activity but a regular and consistent one. Hence, using this budgeting approach will significantly raise your chances of being able to successfully and consistently put money aside for your future needs. This is called the prioritized savings approach, a sample of which can be found in Annex B.

Two Variables Of The Budgeting Equation

A lot of people approach budgeting by focusing only on the expenses variable of the budgeting equation. While this is often enough to at least break even, it isn't the optimal way to ensure that your future needs - and your wants - will be met. There's another variable that - if taken seriously and planned very well - can increase your cash inflows too. It's a cash outflow that can give you more cash inflows – and it's called investments.

In Chapters 4 and 5, we'll talk about budgeting your expenses, i.e., minimizing them, and investing your money so you can have more of it in the future and allow you to take control over your financial future and start really living the life you've always wanted.

CHAPTER 4:

Minimizing Expenses

When it comes to minimizing expenses, there are many different things - usually small ones - that if done right and consistently can add up to substantial savings every month and every year. In this chapter, we'll look at some of the best ways you can minimize your expenses.

Mental Approaches

Mental approaches to budgeting for expenses are perhaps more important than practical ones. If the mindset is not right a person will not be able to sustain any wise and sound financial practice. That is because everything begins in the mind, so if the source isn't right, the output will not be right either. The following are some important mental approaches to effectively budgeting expenses.

Contentment

The single biggest reason why most people are not able to manage their finances well and end up becoming mired in bad debts or worse, become bankrupt, is discontentment. This type of mindset is one that says you *need* to have *more* of what you already have - even if you really don't need them anymore. Take for example clothes.

Many men and women are so obsessed with looking hip, cool, and chic to the point that they are always on shopping sprees even if they can't afford it. One mentality people have is that it's a mortal sin (at least according to the fashion police) to wear the same piece of clothing twice! Think about it, every time you go out in public, you need to wear a different attire and if you don't, the fashion police and their spawns will lambast you in public, even if you look great. Because this is common with celebrities, it puts in the minds of their viewers that wearing the same clothes twice is so uncool and undesirable. And because a lot of people are insecure with themselves, they swallow this lie and want to always buy new clothes to be accepted, or at the very least, not be criticized or rejected.

Another way people are mired in bad debts is electronic gadgets. Never mind if their iPhones are barely a year old and are working perfectly fine.

It would be ideal if you could command yourself to be "content" and all desires to get the newest top-of-the-line gadgets, buy the coolest clothes every month, or take those vacations you really can't afford, will go away. However, you can put yourself in a position where such desires can be weakened to the point where you don't feel unhappy if you don't always get to buy all the things you want when you don't really need them.

All you need is discipline and a desire to change. Set goals and stick to them. Believe me, there is no better feeling than achieving short-term and long-term financial goals, especially when you know it is changing your future for the better. Remember, you are reading this book because you want to improve your bottom line. But for things to change, first you have to change.

Non-Conformity

We can be the most content people in the world, but if we hang out with people who routinely chide us for not having the same things as they have, we put ourselves in positions where we are strongly pressured to conform to the group's norms. Peer pressure can make intelligent people do the dumbest things and similarly can make financially-wise people become reckless with their finances. My advice is this: short-term sacrifices will be far outweighed by long-term gains.

Fear

Studies have shown that fear is often a very strong motivator and teacher. For example, the Filipino overseas workers, collectively known as OFWs, who are able to bear the loneliness of being separated from their families for extended periods of time. The only reason they can do this and really tighten their personal budgets in foreign countries they work in is because of fear that their families back in the Philippines will go hungry and will not be able to have their needs met if they quit their jobs and come home, or if they squander the money they earn while working abroad. They really tighten their belts because they fear the worst may happen financially to their loved ones. So even if many of them aren't financial gurus, they are able to effectively minimize their personal expenses so they can have money to send back home to their families.

Needs Versus Wants

Finally, it's very important that you are able to clearly distinguish between needs and wants. You may find this suggestion to be something that's basic commonsense but believe me, many have fallen financially because of the inability to understand and distinguish needs versus wants, however basic and commonsense this principle is.

If you feel the need to buy something, then ask yourself this. Do I really "need" this? If the honest answer is no then it is a "want" and think of the money you are saving, especially if you will need to borrow money (or use your credit card) to buy it.

Even with your regular grocery shopping the needs versus wants conundrum is still one that causes many people to exceed their budget.

One way to overcome this is to plan your meals a week ahead, then, write out your shopping list with what you need and stick to it.

Resist the temptation to add extras that are not on your list. Try it. You will be amazed at the money you will save over a month….and a year.

Practical Approaches

Now that we've tackled mental approaches to budgeting your expenses, it's time to get practical. Here are just some examples of how you can save money. I'm sure if you are serious about improving your financial future you will be able to come up with a host of ideas of your own.

<u>Keep Records</u>

A keystone habit - according to bestselling author Charles Duhigg in his book *The Power of Habits* - is one that if you acquire or develop will automatically lead to the acquisition of other good habits or the cessation of bad ones. It's like that first domino in a long line of falling dominoes. You tip it and the rest follow. And according to Duhigg, one of them is journaling.

While the context of Duhigg's journaling example in his book was dieting and losing weight, the principle that made it an effective weight loss keystone habit is equally applicable to personal finances. By recording or journaling all your expenses, you will become more and more aware of how you spend your money. And as that happens, chances are high that you will automatically act according to the information you glean from your records.

This can be done easily and inexpensively by using an Excel or Google spreadsheet. Do this for all your expenses and you will have a clear picture of where your money is going. Then, you will be able to work out what you can cut down on and channel the extra money into savings. By simply recording all your expenses you will become much better at budgeting.

Commuting

By commuting, I'm talking about taking the bus, train or other-forms of transport instead of the more expensive forms such as taxis or Uber. Also, it's not just petrol that you'll be paying for when you take your car, there's also associated costs such as tires and servicing, as well as parking expenses. Remember, your goal is the decrease your expenses and increase your savings so every dollar counts.

Carpooling

Let's face it: some places don't have good public transport systems. So if driving is the most effective way to get around, try a carpool. By doing this, you can spread your expenses among several different people - you included - and that can help bring down your personal expenses.

Eat In

Every now and then, especially on special occasions, it's perfectly okay to eat out and celebrate or order in takeaway. But in most cases, the most budget-friendly option is to eat a home-prepared meal.

Consider the fact that restaurants and food stalls operate to make money - they're not charitable institutions - which means they are more expensive than home-cooked meals. And instead of always buying your work lunch, prepare your lunch and snacks at home and save a lot of money. Chances are your meals will be healthier too. Another great option is the cook extra for your dinner the night before and take it for lunch the next day. A crockpot or slow cooker is great for this.

Video-Streaming Services

If you like watching movies, you'll be able to save more money by taking out a subscription to Netflix or some other video-streaming service where, for a low monthly fee, you can watch as many movies, TV shows, and documentaries as you want! The best part is the monthly subscription is practically the same as the cost of a movie ticket, but you get to watch a lot more shows from the comfort of your own home.

Go for Lesser Known Brands

In many instances, the quality of lesser known brands - household supplies, clothes, or electronics – are just as good as their more expensive alternatives.

When it comes to household consumable supplies, the added benefits of more expensive brands compared to lesser-priced ones are hardly noticeable. The only thing you're paying extra for is the brand.

Don't be fooled by advertising and image.

CHAPTER 5:

Investing In Your Future

You may be wondering why investments are an important part of budgeting. Put simply, investments are the means by which you can make your money grow. It's also the means by which - if done right - can make it easier for you to achieve financial security. In this chapter, we'll look at the things you'll need to consider in choosing the best investments based on your goals, risk appetite and financial position.

For example, a financial goal may be to save enough money for a home deposit in four years. So, factoring in inflation, your specific financial goal may be to have $50,000 at the end of four years.

If you already have a mortgage your goal may be to save for an investment property.

Another example of a financial goal is to have enough money to send your new-born son to university by the time he's 18 years old. So again, factoring in inflation, you'll need to have $95,000 to fund his four-year college course. In this case, your specific financial goal is to have $95,000 at the end of 17 years.

Given your specific financial goal, you can choose your investments according to expected average annual rates of return. The higher the expected average annual rate of return, the faster you can accomplish your specific financial goal or the less money you'll have to put in to achieve it within your targeted time frame. The lower the average annual rate of return, the longer it will take you to achieve your specific financial goal or the higher the amount you'll need to invest to achieve it within your specified time frame.

To get a better understanding, here's how to work out how much you'll need to invest now (Present Value) - assuming a one-time investment - at a specific average annual rate of return to accomplish your specific financial goal (Future Value):

$$Present\ Value = Future\ Value \div [1+r]^t$$

Where: r = expected average annual rate of return
t = number of years

Let's say you have a choice between investments A and B, where the average expected annual returns are 9% and 8% respectively. Substituting the numbers we'll get:

Present Value if Investment A = $95,000 \div [1+0.09]^{17}$
Present Value if Investment A = $95,000 \div [1.09]^{17}$
Present Value if Investment A = $95,000 \div 4.3276$
*Present Value if Investment A = **$21,951.95***

Present Value if Investment B = $95,000 \div [1+0.08]^{17}$
Present Value if Investment B = $95,000 \div [1.08]^{17}$
Present Value if Investment B = $95,000 \div 3.7000$
*Present Value if Investment B = **$25,675.55***

With investment A, the higher expected average annual rate of return, you'll have to invest only $21,951.95 today to have an expected value of $95,000 after 17 years, which is your specific financial goal. With investment B, the lower expected average annual rate of return, you'll need to invest a bigger amount today of $25,675.55 to have an expected value of $95,000 by the end of 17 years. So, if we're to base it purely on rate of return, it makes more sense to choose investment A, right? But this is not the only consideration.

Risk

The cardinal principle governing financial investments is this: the higher your expected or desired returns, the higher the financial risk. So, if you're thinking of choosing investment A, you'll need to understand that the expected returns aren't guaranteed and with its higher expected average annual return, its risk is also higher compared to investment B.

What does this mean? It means that the risk for a lower future value is much higher compared to investment B. If you want lower risk, the trade-off is lower potential returns, and therefore a higher investment amount, as you've seen in our example. This is what's commonly referred to in financial circles as the risk-return trade-off.

The least risky financial investments are government securities issued by the Federal Government, and as such, they also have the lowest average annual rate of return, which ranges from 2% to 3% only. They're the least risky because the risk for non-payment is zero as the Federal Government can always print dollars to pay off their debts. On the other hand, the average annual rate of return on United States Stocks as represented by the S&P 500 since its inception in 1928 is about 10%, but there are years when returns are negative -meaning loss instead of gain.

Going back to our example, which of the two investment options should you now choose? If returns are your priority and your risk appetite is high, investment A is your best option. But if your risk appetite or tolerance is low, investment B is your best bet, albeit it will require you to invest more money.

CHAPTER 6:

Paying Off Bad Debts

You won't be able to meet your financial needs and goals if you are drowning in bad debts. So, the most urgent thing you'll need to do to start getting back on track in terms of your personal or family finances, is to pay off your bad debts. Here's how you can prepare a realistic budget for paying off your debts.

Prioritize Debt Payments

If you really want to get out of debt, you will need to make this a priority. This doesn't mean you shouldn't eat just to have money to pay off your debts. It simply means that after your actual needs like food, clothing, utilities and shelter, everything else should go to paying off debts. It's the only way. As the saying goes what gets prioritized gets done. So, unless you prioritize debt payments, you will never pay them off. When you start your budget, all available excess funds should go towards paying off bad debts. When you are (bad) debt-free then you can start saving for the future. However, if your total (bad) debts mean you cannot comfortably maintain the payments, or you want to find a way to pay them off faster, there are some alternative options you may want to consider.

Talk To Your Creditors

Most people with bad debts think that simply ignoring their creditors or worse, running away from them, is the best solution to their debt problems. They are gravely mistaken. Doing so will only make things much worse than they already are. Firstly, it will force their creditors to continue piling on the interest and penalties to their account, burying them further in debt until they become bankrupt. They might think bankruptcy is a great option as it will force creditors to stop harassing them. While that may be the case, their credit scores will be severely affected, and it will be very hard - if not impossible - to borrow money again while bankrupt, or to apply for new utility accounts. And considering it also takes time after coming out of bankruptcy for credit scores to rebound, bankruptcy suddenly loses its appeal.

If someone is currently buried in bad debts, talking to their creditors increases the chances of them putting on hold the accumulation of interest and penalties. Even better, it will make them more open to the possibility of restructuring your debts based on what you can afford to pay so that you can eventually get out of bad debts and minimize the negative impact on your credit scores. Why? Because by taking the proactive step of initiating negotiations, financial institutions will be convinced that you really want to re-pay your debt and the only thing stopping you from doing so is incapacity. When they know you really want to pay them back, trust me, they will look for ways to help you do just that. Let's face it, by helping you there are helping themselves get their money back plus interest.

Sell Or Surrender Assets

One of the quickest ways to pay off your bad debts is to sell some of your assets. Or if your creditors are willing to accommodate, you can surrender acceptable assets in settlement of your bad debts. Only consider assets that will not adversely affect your current needs. As an example, do you have two cars but use one of those most of the time? Is selling one going to have an adverse effect on your current needs or is it simply a luxury? What about that home gym that has been sitting idle in the garage for the past 12 months? Do an inventory of your marketable assets to see if this is a viable option.

Consider Additional Sources Of Income

Cutting down on expenses to free up additional money for paying off bad debts can only go so far because there's such a thing as minimum cost of living, that if you go below will render you unable to meet your (and your family's) needs completely. If you can no longer find any expenses to cut down on, it's time to look for additional sources of income to gradually pay off your bad debts.

Fortunately, there are many side income sources you can get into, from earning a second income from a part-time job, to using skills you have to earn extra income online. On major job-sourcing sites such as UpWork and Fiverr, there are thousands of online gigs that you can do during your free time that can help you earn extra money to pay off your bad debts and save money for your future needs. From bookkeeping to freelance writing to video editing, the list of available jobs that you can do on the side are practically endless. Sign up for a free account with any of these major platforms and start earning income.

CONCLUSION

Thank you for purchasing this book. I hope it has been helpful in teaching you about budgeting and money management. But more than just learning, I hope you will act immediately on what you have learned. Knowledge is only potential power, and to release the power you must apply what you know and have learned. So go ahead, start applying what you learned and be in control of your personal finances by getting out of debt and living life to the max.

Here's to your success!

Annex A: Sample Contingent Savings Approach Budget

Average Monthly Gross Income			$6,250.00
Less: Taxes (U.S. average of 14%)			$875.00
Average Monthly Net Disposable Income			**$5,375.00**

Less:	Amount	% of Total Monthly Expenses	
Housing	$840.00	18%	
Transportation	$750.33	16%	
Household Operating Expenses (Utilities and Consumables)	$589.00	13%	
Household Food	$550.17	12%	
Social Security Contributions	$460.67	10%	
Debt Payments	$437.67	9%	
Healthcare	$302.58	7%	
Entertainment	$213.67	5%	
Cash Contributions	$152.83	3%	
Clothing and Services	$133.67	3%	
Education	$94.83	2%	
Miscellaneous	$55.33	1%	
Personal Care	$50.67	1%	
Total Average Monthly Expenses	**$4,631.42**	**100%**	**$4,631.42**

Net Savings/(Deficit)			**$743.58**

Annex B: Sample Prioritized Savings Approach Budget

Average Monthly Gross Income	**$6,250.00**
Less: Taxes (U.S. average of 14%)	$875.00
Average Monthly Net Disposable Income	$5,375.00
Less: Fixed Amount of Savings	**$1,500.00**
Net Disposable Income	**$3,875.00**

Less:	Amount	% of Total Monthly Expenses	
Housing	$702.81	18%	
Transportation	$627.79	16%	
Household Operating Expenses (Utilities and Consumables)	$492.80	13%	
Household Food	$460.31	12%	
Social Security Contributions	$385.43	10%	
Debt Payments	$366.19	9%	
Healthcare	$253.16	7%	
Entertainment	$178.77	5%	
Cash Contributions	$127.87	3%	
Clothing and Services	$111.84	3%	
Education	$79.34	2%	
Miscellaneous	$46.30	1%	
Personal Care	$42.39	1%	
Total Average Monthly Expenses	**$3,875.00**	**100%**	**$3,875.00**

Made in the USA
Middletown, DE
23 May 2019